rhythms of rebirth

christian bosse

other books by christian bosse

poetry

Thirst
Sojourner
Eyes On You

nonfiction

Arise With Singing
Arise With Singing: Study Guide

this book is dedicated to the ones
who struggle to see the light in themselves
only to fight off the darkness when
they finally discover they have
something to offer

table of contents

you were made to
bud
bloom
wither
prune
blossom

budding

christian bosse

breathe
into my lungs
your breath of life

fill
my soul to the brim
with your grandeur

sow
within me
your abundant beauty

I want to live
where the light pours in
aglow in its glee
my spirit soars
to the melody of
love + grace
intertwined in the golden beams

I want to live
where the light pours in
caressed by its compassion
my soul rests
in the perch of
peace + contentment
woven in the amber glow

I want to live
where the light pours in
unveiled by its honesty
my heart regenerates
in the salve of
mercy + truth
brewed in the honey splendor

I want to live where the light pours in

from dawn to dusk
and in between
I stare at the world
and dream
that what I have to offer
isn't so small
that who I am
is worthy of your call

"blend in,"
I told myself.
"there's no need to stand out,
to look different,
to be unique."

"stay hidden,"
I fussed.
but try as I might,
every part of me
wanted to break free
of the mold

I leap towards the sun
aspiring to harness
its breath-taking power
only to discover what's inside of me
is a supernova waiting to erupt

you knit the melody
stirring in the depths of my soul
a potent concoction
of chords crashing down
on the staves of my heart

uncontainable
the melody you fashioned for me
pours out of every exhale
making every breath
an opportunity to praise

desperate hands
claw at my garment of praise
but I tighten my grip
protecting what's precious

the wind beats upon my back
challenging me to withstand the storm
mocking me as I struggle to grow
in the midst of chaos
but I will not be shaken
I will stand my ground
protecting what's budding beneath the surface

awakening
in the hollows of my spirit
is a force
built to withstand
the strongest of oppressors
threatening to
take control

conceal me
in endless amber fields
of your grace
far away
from the pressures of this world
threatening to bury
the treasure
you bestowed within my heart

rhythms of rebirth

allow yourself
room to grow
far away from the
worms + weeds
that encroach upon
your metamorphosis

awaken
to the blooms
beating at your chest
yearning to erupt
in splendor + grandeur

reach for the sky
permitting your stem
to rise
high above what's ordinary
affirming your heart's cry
to flourish

christian bosse

pour love
into the world
without asking
if anyone deserves it

crowds draw near
to dance to the rhythm
pulsing through your veins
delighting in every beat
empowered by the song of freedom
exuding from your presence

christian bosse

blooming

christian bosse

spring tickles my nose
luring me from my
hiding place
signaling that it's time
to bear witness
of the transformation
taking place in my spirit

do not fear
what's blossoming within you
comes from seeds that were sown
eons ago
when the light was just a spark
and the earth was just beginning

everything has to start somewhere.
this is where you begin.

see for yourself
you are a masterpiece
etched in marble
a work of wonder
not to be hidden
under a veil
not to be deserted
in dark corners

the darkness whispers in my ear
urging me to stay quiet
as it ties me into a bind
I wish it was easy to comply
but this doesn't feel right
this feels upside-down
I shouldn't live my life bound
to the desires of the darkness
when I know it's only
a shadow in the light

you don't have to look like anyone else.

she might be the sea
he might be the sky
but you're a wildfire
burning through the night

don't question your flicker
don't question your flames
you are one-of-a-kind
so live untamed

they might snicker
and stare
but no one knows
how long it took
for you to see the light
radiating inside of you
is a spark worth unveiling

snip the lies
tangling your shoots + leaves
make room for you to grow freely

christian bosse

the tallest flowers
dance in the mud
sing in the sun
blossom unashamed
and shed a petal or two
not caring who sees

the tallest of flowers
grow unapologetically

take every apology
you've made for being who you are
and bury them behind the tool shed

let your petals
blossom
in the morning light
for all to see
and do so without
remorse

wildflowers don't ask for permission.
they grow wherever they will.

let courage rise
from the depths of your spirit
strengthening you to glow
in authentic brilliance

all the petals within you
waited until now to bloom
so let yourself bloom
fascinating colors
let yourself fulfill
every prophesy
spoken over you

don't hold on to what's inside of you.
let it pour and pour and pour until your world is filled with
beauty.

fill this dismal world
with all the colors of your rainbow
let your heart bleed wonder
turning heads at the sight
of your pure artistry

there is no future
there is no past
only a series of
now
step into each moment
unashamed
ready to share the riches
concealed within you

seasons come and go. summer won't last forever. don't miss your opportunity to flourish.

christian bosse

wilting

christian bosse

suddenly
the sun waved its final goodbye
letting the night settle in

without warning
I withered
my crumpled petals
whisked away
in the wind
lost in the unknown
there I remain
empty

beyond the warmth
of the light
my leaves shivered
curling under me
searching for some form
of comfort
in the coolness of night

weathered layers
of my ragged skin
collect on the threshing floor
awaiting restoration

seasons of sifting
leave me bare
pieces of me divided
with no hope of redemption

change corroded my joy
like a rushing river
in the canyon of my soul

day by day
pieces of me
shriveled
like ashes
dispersed
unable to be
salvaged

the world gazes
in excitement
at the stardust you shed
never knowing the pain
you endured
to yield such a prize

every flower sheds its petals.

pressed between
words unspoken
I craved the light
my petals stretched
aching for relief
to no avail
crushed under the weight
of the pages

caged
the bird grows comfortable
sitting on its perch
no longer dreaming
of open skies
no longer marveling
at creation
no longer hungry
for freedom
simply tame
caged

my knees buckle
unable to bear the burdens
piled upon my back

silently
I crouched
under the weight
of the world
crying in agony
desperate for some sign of
reprieve

you weren't meant to bear every weight stacked on your
shoulders.

christian bosse

pruning

christian bosse

life stabbed at my stem
snipping my strength
cutting me down to nothing
exposing all my weaknesses

christian bosse

you press
every tender wound
making me bleed
all over again

rhythms of rebirth

each day brings new
trials
each season brings new
burdens

the sun created a mural on the wall
dedicating its art to me
my heart sank into the floor
no sunlight could warm
my indigo soul

my body
fell into an abyss
and I let it slip
I let it slip
no strength left
to evade the pit
I fell right in
I fell right in

a torrential downpour
drenched my tattered soul
stripping me down to nothing

every burden
crashed down on my shoulders
eradicating what hope I had left

raw from the
onslaught of life
I stand exposed
with nothing to offer
but the remnants
of who I once was

christian bosse

I opened the door
and waited for grief to leave
but there he remained
on my couch
making himself at home

winter settled in
a blanket to cover my dry bones
I let it bury me
and went into hibernation
uncertain I'd rise again

find the courage to withstand the pruning process.
it may be brutal, but you will survive.

let every piece of you
fall apart

christian bosse

spill your pain
across blank pages
paying no mind to
let the ink dry

spill
spill
spill
until there's no ink left
pour it all out
leaving nothing unsaid

lean into your pain
letting your soul
come face-to-face
with what's burying you alive

christian bosse

stare into your eyes
search the depths of your identity
taking everything in

meet yourself halfway
taking each step of faith
towards transparency
vulnerability
and healing

"the end,"
I cried,
lifting my hands in dismay
little did I know
the end was actually
the beginning

a pool of tears
sank into the cracks
of the floorboards
as I collected
the fragments
of who I was
somehow my soul
trusted the miracle
that even this could be
redeemed

christian bosse

throw your gaze
towards the horizon
and believe
you will outgrow this season

slipping between my fingers
were the remnants of the season
my face crinkled in despair
convinced it was the end
I turned back against the wind
only to come face-to-face
with the beginning

though darkness loomed
hope arose with the dawn
quieting all anxieties
in steady tranquility

winds of change
strip my face bare
taking snippets of my heart
adrift in the gale

a makeshift mask
enshrouding my skin
conceals my nakedness
from the world

the shelter of solitude
draws me from my façade
pacifying my fears
one-by-one

christian bosse

the crisp air hums music in my ears
beckoning me to draw close
to embrace the season
with a heart abounding in gratitude

wholeheartedly accepting its invitation
I glean from its wisdom
relinquishing all control
with halfhearted courage

whispered wishes
take flight in the flurries
twirling in the winter air

frigid temperatures
couldn't discourage
the warmth swelling inside

christian bosse

.

rebirth

christian bosse

down I plunged
into the depths of despair
ready to drown in
my every sorrow
but you plucked me up
out of the abysmal waters
saving me from myself
once again

I searched the
ends of the earth
seeking sanctuary in
ordinary things

lo and behold
you are the shelter
I needed most

sometimes, we can't rescue ourselves.

christian bosse

ripples of joy
shake the darkness inside
commanding my downcast soul
to rise in gratitude

shifting seasons
bring new glories
like little love notes
affectionate + pure

waltzing whirlwinds
bring new promises
like unprecedented psalms
unrivaled + true

the sun tickled my nose
a sweet hello from creation
rang in my ears
morning greeted me like a
friend

the new day was a blessing
not a burden

refreshing raindrops
sing lullabies of peace
serenading the stirring heart
into a deep slumber

amiss in reverie
bliss overcomes the soul
entertaining with the gift of play
reviving innocence + wonder

conquered
chaos flees the heart
yielding to the authority of peace
confounded by its power

murmuring thunder
recites vows of hope
awakening the steady heart
to reign again

christian bosse

new revelations settle in
like the morning dew
on the shallow of my mind

you are the promise
sending shockwaves
of peace
through my body

breaking ground
in my calloused heart
faith springs forth

rediscovering hope is like gaining a second wind. it propels you to run farther, longer, and with more energy than ever before. don't underestimate the power of hope.

you sew every wound
shut
giving me a chance to truly
heal

clinched fist
held on to the shattered fragments
of my heart
but you murmured music in my ears
encouraging me to let it all go
and live

rhythms of rebirth

exhale
releasing from your lungs
the impurities that settled there
threatening to snuff out
all of your oxygen

christian bosse

cast aside
every burden
hanging like a noose
around your neck
and dance in freedom

healing happens when you're honest. when you strip away the disguise and see yourself fully, you begin the healing process. you embrace life – no matter how ugly it is – and are rewarded with renewal and restoration.

you will shed
every layer
until you're nothing
but bones

fear not –

you will rebuild
from this place
stronger than before;
a fortress of stone

seek the light
and drink it in
filling your veins
with vitality
restoring your soul
back to health

my voice rose
like the dawn
a gentle murmur
of powder blue + pink
splashed upon the horizon

in newfound boldness
I spoke up
sending ripples
of gold, tangerine + magenta
across the sky
in blazing glory

forgive yourself

emerging from the
muck + mire
to bloom your way
takes courage,
tenacity + resilience

christian bosse

glimmers of light
pierce through the cracks
of my cocoon
persuading me to
emerge from my shell

leaving behind what's dead
I break forth in victory
conquering my past
in joyous anticipation
of the future

pledge to be
fully you
even when the lights go dim
and all that's left
is a twinkling in the distance

pledge to be
fully you
even when pleasure runs out
and all that's left
is your determination to grow

you wouldn't have known your strength if it wasn't for the
elements shaking you down your roots.

don't apologize
for blooming
for wilting
or for anything in between

allow yourself
to bloom again
stretching your leaves
unafraid
of the threat of shears
poised to prune you again

unravel yourself
from the weeds of life
creating space
to obey the call to
blossom

tiny flower buds
broke from the soil
of my hardened heart
coming alive
to the sound of
new promises
whispered by the dawn

though the winter was bleak
it didn't overtake you.

spring is here
it's time to rise again.

lavish yourself
head-to-toe
in grace + forgiveness
healing every wound
with tender love + mercy

feed yourself
unconditional love
unlimited grace
immeasurable mercy
endless forgiveness
fertilizing your spirit
to bear new blooms

life is a perpetual cycle of metamorphosis. we travel through each season experiencing the greatest joys and the cruelest heartbreaks because we are on a life-long journey of growth.

it may be unbearable at times to wilt, molt, or be pruned, but it's worth the next season of blooming.

freedom will not catch you by surprise.
you have to claw it out of the mud.

the sky hurled buckets of rain
upon my back
the winds shook me to the core
the pruning shears slashed my petals
'til I was merely a stem
but nothing could stop me
from spreading my leaves
sprouting new life again

rhythms of rebirth

christian bosse

about the author

Photo taken by Laura Campbell

Christian Bosse is a Christian author, poet and mentor. Writing is her life-long method of self-care and creative expression. She loves to help others find healing, revelation, and transformation through God via her books and one-on-one coaching sessions.

She's a Kansas City native and currently resides there with her husband and daughters. When she isn't writing or mentoring, Christian is spending quality time with her family and loved ones.

Christian love to connect on social media. You can find her at bychristianbosse.com or on Instagram, Twitter and Pinterest @christianbosse_

christian bosse

Made in the USA
Las Vegas, NV
05 January 2021

15218134R00081